The Accidental Project Manager 2.0

Go beyond theory to simplify project management and deliver results.

For my family who supported this crazy idea of a book.

Table of Contents

Part 1   3

    Being an accidental project manager   4

    Beware of the leadership void   15

    Simplification leads to results   22

    Initiating change   28

    Effective planning   36

    It's all about execution   45

    The trap of administrative excellence   59

    Closing the project   66

    Project management simplified   71

    Simplified toolkit   77

    Putting it all together   93

Part 2   99

Why focus on execution   102

Focusing on the right things   108

Influencing change Part 1   115

Influencing change Part 2   124

Typical sticking points   128

Building high performing teams   137

Risk identification & mitigation   142

Modern change management   145

Conclusion   154

Recommended reading   156

Journal   158

The Accidental Project Manager 2.0

Part I

Welcome Accidental Project Manager to 2.0!

In the first version of this book, I tried to create a framework that would help people simplify project management and to understand why that is so important. While I think it was a good start, the truth is an idea is nothing without the means to apply it to your life and actually use it when needed. In fact, that is where many theories go off track. They have great talking points and buzzwords, but often come up short in practical application.

In this new version, I have added elements for practical application including reflection points and a journal along with ideas for building teams, improving influencing and modern change management. This is not meant to be a one-stop solution for every project or process initiative, but rather a guide to help you on your journey.

Being an accidental project manager

I never intended to become a project manager.

While I always enjoyed working on special projects, the idea of doing that full time just wasn't part of my master plan. That is not to diminish the value of project management, I just didn't think it was for me. Wow, I could not have been more wrong and as luck would have it, I would be able to test that theory very quickly.

When my post-college career began, I was in business operations and enjoyed leading a small team that had a big impact on the growth of my business unit. As the business grew beyond the original organizational plan, I was approached by my boss at the time to lead an initiative that would redesign the complete end-to-end process for loan origination and servicing. Once complete, this process would be more scalable to support our growth. To be clear, this wasn't a special, new role but rather it was in addition to my day job.

We had a tight deadline to accomplish this, 45 days to be exact, before the third quarter close. In addition to the process overhaul, we had to hire around twenty people to fill newly designed roles. It would be challenging to find the right skill set for a team this size with such diverse needs without the time crunch or the process change. It was also critical to find people that could fit the culture. Background, skills and education were important, but we needed people that wanted to learn, contribute and be willing to look at things from a fresh perspective.

Needless to say, these requirements made for some really long days.

It was 2002 and I worked for GE Capital which was immersed in Six Sigma at the time. Everyone was leading some type of project, attending training or both to gain certification so they could add it to their resume. It was less about making effective changes as it was about checking the box to get certified and list that as an accomplishment for the year. Truthfully, most of the so called "projects" were just cover for previously determined business decisions, but that is another story.

As I began my journey into the realm of process improvement, I realized that the standard quality tools were not easily adaptable to process design. While very effective in manufacturing, they seemed quite clunky for process changes in a service business. I wasn't a project manager by trade, but rather an Operations guy trying to keep multiple plates spinning at the same time. Pushing my frustration aside, I thought there had to be a simpler way to leverage project management tools as an "accidental project manager".

Before we go on with the story, I must pause for a moment to actually define the term "accidental project manager". What exactly do I mean?

They exist in every organization and are often overlooked, not supported or both. They are everyday managers, professionals or executives that are tasked with some type of non-technical strategic initiative or project to improve or design a process, optimize workforce alignment or a whole host of items in addition to their "day" job. Often times, they struggle to find effective tools and training that are easy to use and allow them to convey planning and results to senior leadership.

That is where this book fits. When I was learning project management, there was no guide or simplified toolkit to help me. It was either leading to a certification of some sort or focused on technology projects. Neither are bad, in and of themselves, but I needed something that a non-project manager could use to help with project management. I didn't need countless pages on work breakdown structures or how to formulate the perfect problem statement. I needed something practical to use as a reference. That something didn't exist, so I decided to write the book that I would have liked 10+ years ago.

I want to help you lead successful projects and process change initiatives using simple, time tested and business proven tools and techniques. This is about execution and getting things done rather than pretty Gantt charts and PowerPoint decks. If you want to learn about that, you will need a different book.

The tools and techniques in this book have been used in companies of all sizes and took me years to compile into a process that was useable. To be sure these are not new discoveries, but rather lessons from my years of trial and error for the best way to implement consistent, scalable process changes and deliver results on non-technology projects.

Now, back to the story...

We worked through most of late July and August to design the new organization while continuing to close deals and execute on day to day operations. By late August, we had simplified our operations process and trained the existing team on the changes. From there we engaged them throughout the interview process with potential candidates. We launched our new process approximately three weeks before quarter close and on-boarded our team members shortly after launch.

Needless to say, it was not an optimal quarter close, but we got through it, learned many lessons and made process adjustments along the way. It was then that I learned that true process optimization and project management didn't end when the project closed rather it was an ongoing journey of continuous improvement. It was not limited to achieving a certification or designation, but rather a means to change the game. In fact, we never stopped making adjustments as conditions and customer expectations continued to evolve.

Everyday Project Management

During my career, I had the privilege of leading teams and building processes within multiple functions. I learned many skills and different perspectives from each role. Along the way, I found that the most important thing wasn't the tools used or the book that I referenced, but that I needed to build sustainable changes because I was the one who had to live with it.

Truthfully, I think that is an element that is lacking in modern project management. We live in a world of centralized project offices (aka PMOs) and consultants that can push projects along, but really don't have to live with the results once the project is closed. They are on to the next project, initiative or client.

Now, don't get me wrong, I am not throwing stones, (well, maybe a few small ones), but I think that is why change management initiatives are less effective than they could be once completed. As a functional leader also responsible for driving sustainable, profitable change, I chose to engage my team in the project and be part of designing the solution. I wanted those closest to the process and to the customer to have input in creating a solution so we knew precisely what would work or not. As a result, my team was engaged and owned the change throughout the project and beyond.

That is the magic potion for successful projects. Nothing fancy or cutting edge, just common sense. Here are a few of my rules for successful project management:

1. Involve your best and brightest early and often.
2. Build your change around the long-term direction – look beyond the current project and see how this will impact operations, customers and users down the road.
3. Don't be the smartest person in the room – if you are you have the wrong people in the room!
4. Delegate and empower your team – they know what needs to be done, give them the chance to do it.

5. Hold people accountable for decisions – find out the why behind the choice and use it to coach and develop your team into leaders.
6. Don't eat the whale – break the project into manageable chunks once you understand the picture and the project goals.

Remember, this is about getting sustainable results. You will need a strong team to create lasting change. Far too often people only look at their own process when making a change and think nothing about the impact to another team. Eventually when the other team gets tired of additional work or an inferior process, they start a project of their own and the work ends up shifting somewhere else in the business. By developing and nurturing cross-functional relationships from the start, you can prevent this cycle from starting.

There are many critical elements to a successful business and a successful project. None of them play as much of a role as leadership. The funny thing about leadership is that it doesn't have to come from someone with a title. It can come from anywhere in the organization, but we typically only look for it from Senior Managers or CEOs. I am not sure why we started to do that, but it has to be more grassroots than that. It has to start with the individual. Senior leaders can and should provide the overall vision, but then should allow their people to execute in the best way possible to create a culture of sustainable change and learning.

The key point, regardless of industry, is that leadership cannot be delegated or outsourced. Leaders must lead. No excuses and no short cuts. It is not about being popular. It is about tough choices, engaging strategy and empowering your best people to drive the organization forward.

That said, we are seeing a lack of leadership in many companies today and that is impacting their business. At the time of this writing, there are a few iconic brands that are struggling to prepare for the future or lost altogether. Leadership makes the difference and can create clarity for the future in an uncertain world. At best, a lack of leadership creates confusion and frustration. At worst, it leaves your team in a void lacking a clear vision or direction.

Beware of the leadership void

"Be the yard stick of quality. Some people are not used to an environment where excellence is expected."

- Steve Jobs

Regardless of industry, many of us feel the impact of alleged leaders that are unwilling or unable to provide true leadership. Think about your own organization for a moment. How engaged are senior leaders in change initiatives beyond faster, cheaper, lower headcount, etc.?

There is a growing leadership crisis that is the root cause of lower morale, higher turnover, higher costs and poor customer experience. At the time of this writing, we live in a world of growing uncertainty. Leadership should provide stability in an ever changing and disruptive corporate landscape, but unfortunately, they are not delivering consistently.

With all of this in play, we enter a void where there is no clear direction, conflicting or constantly changing priorities or absolute silence. Put simply, it is a lack of genuine leaders who act with vision and determination regardless of what people think of them or what is popular. Genuine leaders do what needs to be done to move the company forward and continually add value to shareholders and customers. It is not about what an analyst thinks or what is trendy, but rather to progressively move toward a worthy ideal.

Think about Dwight D. Eisenhower, Alan Mulally, J.P. Morgan, Franklin Roosevelt, Winston Churchill and many others. History is filled with people who were true leaders and took care of business when their company, country or world needed them the most. Regardless of what you may think of the people listed above, you cannot deny their ability to lead and unite people toward a common goal.

Unfortunately, at the time of this writing, we are in a period where that simply doesn't happen. Our politicians govern via sound bites rather than through sound policy. They try to one up each other or send social media blasts to appeal to the lowest common denominator. Business leaders fail to provide a clear strategic vision and then jump ship when the going gets tough. Employees feel uninspired at best or like easily replaceable resources at worst. No big goals or strategic thinking, just maintaining the status quo.

Rather than preserving the status quo, we should be using technology and increased connectivity to set big goals and transform the world as we have done many times in the past. The secret of big goals is it energizes people and can empower them to do great things. It encourages them to think big and contribute beyond their everyday job duties. A great leader can take average and make it extraordinary.

There is a reluctance to take big swings that could improve society or add shareholder value. Instead, we live with small, easily achievable goals and nothing too big or controversial. Today's so-called leaders live for the next quarter or the next news cycle. Companies are full of disengaged employees who are waiting for the next layoff or reduction in benefits. We have no cause, no big rock to move and as a result people grow complacent and comfortable with the status quo.

It is time for that to change.

First, it is time for people need to wake up, come back to the real world and demand personal excellence from themselves to live an extraordinary life. Next, it is time we demand the same from our leaders and if they cannot deliver that consistently then we need to replace them. Finally, we must stop treating the symptoms of poor leadership and focus on the root cause which is the tolerance of poor leadership.

You don't have to be a politician or a CEO to be a leader. Leadership starts with you, right now, wherever you are. Seize the moment; take advantage of the opportunity to bring out the best in yourself, in others and in the world. The world needs leadership more now than ever before.

Change begins in subtle ways and across all levels of an organization. You do not have to be an executive to critically examine your business processes and simplify them, but change does start with leadership (formally or informally). There is no way around that. Leadership is the critical element for successful change.

Think about these questions for a moment:

Why do change initiatives fail?

Why do people and processes revert to the old way of doing things rather than looking ahead to the future?

Why do people get stuck without a clear path forward?

The common theme in all of these questions is a lack of leadership. It does not begin with a job title, but it could be reinforced by one. Leaders should set the direction and the overall vision for the organization but cannot do everything on their own. To be truly effective, they should then leave it to the talented people on their teams and in their organization to chart the course and execute on that strategy. Begin with the future in mind, but don't obsess about details. Provide the direction and then empower your teams to execute. Leadership drives empowerment and accountability at all levels of the organization. Leadership is about visualizing the future and then getting the best out of your people to move the organization forward. Leadership is about playing to your strengths and those of your team. Leadership is about tough decisions and celebrations.

True leadership is a skill that never gets replaced or outsourced. It is desperately needed globally. It is often underappreciated yet very noticeable when it is missing.

Leadership sets the standard and is the compass for the organization. Become the leader you wish you had. Demonstrate to people what excellence looks like and motivate them to follow your example. Leverage the mountain of experience and knowledge you already possess and go forth to be the leader you always wanted and the one your company needs.

Simplification leads to results

"Our life is frittered away by detail. Simplify, simplify."

- Henry David Thoreau, Walden and Other Writings

If you have ever built a process from the ground up or spent time reengineering an existing process, you know that sometimes the typical project management methodology and tools seem more complicated than the original problem. Trust me, if you have felt that you are not alone. As I was going through multiple weeks of Six

Sigma training, I thought there had to be a better, simpler way for non-project managers to manage projects. Furthermore, I noticed that not only did most change initiatives fail, but in times of stress people defaulted back to the original process. As a result, the same teams were going through working sessions and process design sessions to fix the same problems over and over again.

As a result of my frustration, I decided to create a simplified framework that could be used to drive consistent results when designing a new process, aligning resources or reengineering an existing process. In order to solve for the future, you need to first understand where you are today. If you do not know how a process works today or the current risks associated with current state, how on earth can you expect to improve it?

Below is the methodology I have cobbled together through years of research and practical use to create lasting, sustainable change within teams and organizations. It begins with a candid assessment of the current state process, environment, technology, resources, etc. Based on that assessment, you can begin the design for a future state that builds upon what is working well, fixes what is not working today while identifying the tools and resources needed for tomorrow. These are not meant to be checkpoints, but rather a guide as you move through a project or process implementation.

As with any methodology, there are key deliverables at each stage so that you can validate if you are on the right trail or heading for the cliff. By having those deliverables clearly defined, you not only have a measuring stick to demonstrate progress, but you are able to assign tasks to the members of the project team. These deliverables should be linked to your project objectives and can also form the basis of your critical path milestones.

Regardless of industry or project type, there are some basic project phases that you will want to leverage to ensure that you incorporate pulse checks throughout your project to confirm the direction. This also breaks things up in a logical manner and allows you to optimize resource allocation rather than have everyone all the time (which doesn't happen in the real world). While most project management training has these phases in some form, I wanted to keep things simple and focused, so here they are....

Initiation - Planning - Execution - Close

That's it...four phases. As with other things in life, more is not better. If your business has multiple phases beyond this, don't just blindly follow along. If they don't fit your project, don't force a fit. It is valuable to determine what would fit, use that and skip the rest. In most cases (not all), they are generic tollgates that apply generally to all projects whether they fit or not.

With any critical initiative we need to identify what we are working on, why people should care, who we need to help us, how we get it done and when it will be complete. Think about it like this, we want to tell people what, so what, now what. If you can do that, you will be able to clearly articulate what the project means to the business, how it will provide benefits in the long term and how you get to the desired result.

If you were to match my hybrid methodology with a more traditional project tollgate structure, it would look something like this:

Initiation	Plan	Execute	Close
Assessment	Determine Strategy	Design	Measure results
Deconstruct current process	Identify resources needed	Build	Plan for continuous improvement
		Test	
		Implement	

Still with me or did you skip to the end? If you are, let's talk about the deliverables and tools for each phase starting with the beginning…Initiation.

Initiating change

"Begin at the beginning, go until you come to the end, then stop".

- Anonymous

When your project is starting, you need to know the goals, the benefits and the why behind the change. If you don't, you are destined for problems. Truthfully, I think "know the why" is an over-utilized term in business today, but it is critical to align business goals or strategic deliverables to the project. Once people understand how a project can positively impact them, they are more likely to support it. Failure here will literally impact funding, the ability to obtain the right resources or simply high-level reinforcements (when needed) which could be the difference between success and failure if an obstacle arises.

By linking the why of the project to a critical or strategic business goal, you now make it important to senior leadership. In doing this, it becomes a priority to someone who can help you when needed, but also makes you accountable for results. It is kind of a double-edged sword but trust me you will like the alternative far less.

This is the first test of your influencing skills (more on that later). As a project manager, you need to be able to bring people together under a common goal. This can be especially difficult when the resources you need do not report to you. That is why it is so important to align your project with organizational needs, especially if there is a cross-functional impact. Building up influencing skills takes time, but once you have your coalition, it is much easier to move the big rocks and get the needed resources. Influencing skills will play a huge role throughout your project. It is a critical skill to get anything done. Cross-functional stakeholders DO NOT care about your charter, process maps or project artifacts. They DO care about process simplification, improving resource capacity and growing revenue. If you can link your deliverables to these types of goals, your path to building a strong coalition becomes much easier.

Next to requirements, I would argue that the initiation phase is the most critical to the overall success of the project. Think of it like the foundation of a house. If the builder uses the wrong materials or forgets to include something, it will get very expensive very quickly to fix the mistake down the road. If your builder misses something when they pour the foundation or at the early stages of the build, how much confidence would you have in their ability to complete the rest of the house? I think the answer is fairly obvious on that one.

By taking a little extra time in the Initiation phase, you will be able to go fast in the long run. Resist the urge to move quickly through this part of the project and be sure to temper the excitement of over-eager sponsors. This "slowness" allows project teams to ensure they are charging after the right goal and will significantly reduce the risk of costly mistakes later. Make no mistake about it; changes, errors and omissions will happen. No project is smooth and flawless every step of the way. However, by taking the time up front to get a complete view of the current state and clearly define the project goals and objectives, you will set yourself up for greater success long term and maintain your own credibility.

Conditions change and process elements reveal things that you may not have known or thought about at the start. Going back to the house analogy for a moment, if you have ever renovated a room in an old house, you know there are always surprises lurking in the walls. The same can be said for historic processes. There are always unwritten rules or exceptions that are not formally documented only understood by people in the organization. You want to uncover these and account for them to the best of your ability. That is why it is important to deconstruct the current state and ensure you have enough time to do it properly. Talk with the people who use the process every day; they will tell you how things really are. Changes and surprises don't have to derail an entire initiative if your preparation takes that chance into account. This mindset will help you as you start planning milestones and key deliverables down the road.

If you take nothing else away from this section, remember one thing…it is always easier, cheaper and faster to correct things early on in a project. If something is ignored, hidden or buried until the end, it is a painful process to make corrections whether it be a process, product or technology initiative.

As you will discover as we move along on this journey, I am fan of simple. To me simple and effective go hand in hand. Just because the project charter is seven pages long, doesn't mean it is a better document. I have seen plenty of garbage project charters in my life that were quite long and wordy. More is not always better. You are looking for thorough and effective with a focus on execution. By using simple tools and templates, you change the focus from completing the form to completing the project.

In my view, simple has many tangible benefits. It is scalable and sustainable. You can build upon simple (if needed). Simple is easy to implement, understand and report on. Complex only gets people confused, but it does look great on PowerPoint (hopefully you detected that note of sarcasm). Remember, we want to be busy executing, not just busy doing busy work. If you overcomplicate the project documentation, your project results will be sub-optimal. Why? Because you are no longer focused on the results, but rather on the administrative minutia. But I digress, more on that later.

Thinking about it another way, if you like to cook, you have probably heard the expression that it is easier to add ingredients than subtract. The same can be said about a process. If you make things overly complex from the start, it is hard to document, control and improve. When this happens, most people don't know what the hell they are supposed to do. They just sit in the meeting and nod then go back to their cubes and complain. We have all experienced that first hand and if you haven't, you are probably the one doing it.

Key deliverables following this phase include:

1. **Initial Assessment** – Think at a high level about the basic reasons for the project or initiative. Why are we starting this project? What are we trying to solve, fix or improve? How do we think we can do it? What impact could it have on the organization or the customer or quality as a whole?
2. **Project Charter** - Simple is best: capture objectives, scope, measurements of success, resources needed and a preliminary timeline
3. **Communication Plan** – Who will you talk to, when will you talk to them and how will you inform them?
4. **Projected timeline** – When will you start, when will you end and what are the early milestones?

Now that we have our prep work completed, let's talk about the next critical step...planning.

Effective planning

"Give me six hours to chop down a tree and I will spend the first four sharpening the axe."

— Abraham Lincoln

Back to our house building analogy for just a moment, because I haven't finished wearing that example out yet. Typically, the builder will provide some type of blueprint or plan to demonstrate they grasp what needs to be done. The builder will then make sure they have all of the materials, contractors and permits needed to complete the build on time.

Same concept here. In the planning phase, you want to build on the information from the initiation phase to align resources, deliverables, tasks and deadlines to ensure your project meets the stated objectives. Project Sponsors and Senior Leadership will be watching the progress at this point because you have made them aware of the issue. In order to effectively launch your initiative, you will need to spend some time in the planning phase.

It starts with understanding the current state of the process you are trying to improve. If you do not get to the root cause of the issue, you will find that you are merely treating symptoms leading to a less than optimal result. Start your current state assessment by mapping the process as it occurs today. For this you will want to engage those closest to the process (i.e. people who do it every day). You are not mapping the process as you hope it would be or how you think it should be. You are mapping it as it is, no matter how ugly. Remember this is not the time to solution. If something appears to be the answer, note it and refer back to it, but don't let it drive the project at this point.

Far too often project managers start this conversation at too high of a level. Executives will tell you how they think a process works. A department head will tell you how the process should work (based on their metrics). But the person who works the process every day will tell you exactly <u>how</u> it really works (usually in great detail) and what they have to do to get things done. That is the detail you want and need. That is where you find the areas of opportunity.

As in other phases, influencing will play a key role in your success moving through this phase. Remember earlier when I said that the only element more important than initiation in a project was requirements? Well, here we are. This is the foundation of the house. This is where all the work from the current state analysis forms the basis of your roadmap to the future state. You need to understand what happens today, why it happens and who makes it happen. In some cases, you may even need to know who is impacted by the process and at what point.

You may be thinking that you should just be able to ask, but it is rarely that easy. As you read in the previous chapter, process changes are seldom clean and easy. If they were, you wouldn't be leading a project or reading this book. They are messy and, in many cases, get screwed up because people fail to document business requirements. Similar to a technology project, you want to have a clear understanding of what people need to do their jobs and meet customer expectations. That is the minimum. Without that, the only certainty is that your solution will most likely flop. The truth is you need to dig deeper and understand not only what work is done but how it is done and how it moves through the current process. This is the heart of the process. If you truly understand this piece, you can successfully deconstruct the true pain points.

You are looking for sustainable change, not just a quick, check the box exercise. Remember to document your process and your requirements, check for understanding and make sure you have uncovered any unwritten or undocumented process elements. One important tip that I will continue to stress throughout this book:

Talk to the people who actually do this and understand it. You will obtain a wealth of knowledge and save a lot of pain later in the project.

Some key deliverables in this phase include:

1. **Requirements Documentation:** This includes your current state assessment and process maps. Document the key inputs, outputs and systems used in the current process. Determine what, if any, workarounds exist and understand the process for managing exceptions. Be able to answer what elements are process critical, what is optional along with potential opportunities.
2. **Risk Assessment**: What risks exist or could potentially impact the project (short term / long

term)? It is not enough to document risks alone, you want to be able to project the likelihood of occurrence as well as the potential severity if they do occur. Once you know that, you can work with the project team or other stakeholders to talk about potential mitigation strategies. If you know your risks, you will want to look for ways to address them or make them less impactful to the process. That is part of a mitigation plan which should be part of any risk assessment. Do not just tell someone about a potential problem, but rather tell them how you intend to address it if it occurs.

3. **Resource Needs**: Who will you need to work on this project, how long will you need them, what will they contribute? You need to make sure that the resources you need are available when you need them and for the duration of their tasks. The last thing you want is a critical resource being pulled off your project and on to something else. That will definitely kill your timeline. If you are

unable to obtain the needed resources, that must be addressed immediately. Do not move forward hoping that you will get them in time. Resources are not easier to get as the project progress and a lack of commitment will impact your timeline.

4. **Project Timeline**: It is time to go beyond the initial projection. In this deliverable, you will want to outline the specific milestones, phase completion and delivery dates. Be sure to list any assumptions that you make in determining project dates, because if/when something changes, you will want to be able to articulate how you came to the original schedule. You will want to build your timeline starting with the final goal and work backward. As you build your timeline, be sure to incorporate some buffer time to allow for unforeseen delays. _Be very clear about what you will deliver and when you will deliver it. Sponsors and Senior Leadership will use this as the measurement of success and/or progress._

5. **Cost/Benefit Analysis**: This can be a tricky component to nail down especially with process improvement projects. Clearly you want to demonstrate an increased effectiveness, but you want to avoid linking efficiency to headcount reduction. That doesn't mean lie, but you want to account for key success factors that are relatively easy to measure and are often overlooked. Rather than align your business case to things outside of your control, look at some non-traditional measures of success that could be controlled by your process. Some examples include: reduced cycle time, improved customer experience, improved quality / error reduction and reduced operational or compliance risk to name a few.

As you can see and probably feel, the need for increased documentation, clear benefits and scheduling increases in the planning phase. The entire goal of this phase can be summarized in three words… Prepare for

Execution. Failure to properly plan will result in failure or suboptimal implementation down the road.

Once you have your schedule set, resources in place, risks documented (including a mitigation plan), requirements detailed and desired benefits documented, it is time to move on to the tough part...Execution.

It's all about execution

"Execute every act of thy life as though it were thy last."

–Marcus Aurelius

Execution. This is where the rubber meets the road. I don't want to make it sound like this is all that matters, but change doesn't happen by planning and strategy alone. Execution is what gets things done.

Let's walk through what we have accomplished so far in our project. At initiation, we identified the problem we need to solve and defined the project goals and deliverables. In planning, we completed a deep dive into the current state, aligned our resources and documented our timeline. Those elements will now form the groundwork for effective execution.

Truthfully, this is where most non-IT projects skid off the road. People become distracted by their day job or obsessed with administrative excellence (more on that mess later) that they fail to actually get anything accomplished. Project success is not measured by the color on your status report or your tollgate results, but rather in the value derived from the end results. If you have a stellar project that was all green and flew through every tollgate, but no one uses what you built, it was a colossal waste of time. I know you checked all the boxes, but there was a clear failure to execute and that includes effective implementation.

So, how do you execute? How can you go from the illusion of execution to actually getting things done? It is really simple actually. In fact, it is so simple that it almost seems incorrect.

It starts by realizing that you will not solve every problem all at once. Big changes seldom are the result of one big swing. Rather it is the sum of many small, simple steps that lead to progressive change. Focus on results, drive improvement and collect small wins as you go. That is all you need to get some momentum and start moving the needle. To be blunt, sometimes you will need to babysit people, be a pain in the ass and a coach all at the same time. But eventually through the follow up, coaching and patience, you teach other people to deliver on their commitments and you are able to hold them accountable if they don't.

This is the magical balance of empowerment and accountability. Everyone wants empowerment, but they try like hell to avoid the accountability part of the equation. Both of those elements are absolutely critical in driving execution in the project and beyond. Without them, the project will feel like you are pushing a big, heavy rock up a really tall hill.

Key deliverables during the execution phase include:

1. **Design Document:** Whether process or system, you will need to design your solution and obtain approval from key stakeholders. This could be a system diagram, process map or blueprint.
2. **Change Requests:** Maybe you need these, maybe you don't. Most projects face some sort of change at some point. It could be a change in scope, change in funding or change in timeline. Anything that deviates from your original, approved project charter should be reflected in a change request. Be mindful that change requests can also lead to scope creep. Scope creep is where things get added over time that increase the project expense and / or duration. I am not saying that all changes lead to scope creep, but just to make you aware that they could.

3. **Test Plans / Results:** Outline and define what you will be testing, who will be testing and how long testing will last. Include results to show defects identified and remediation. Yes, it is a process and yes you will want to test it.

4. **Pilot Plan:** Whether process or technology, a pilot can build upon the lessons learned during testing to ensure that the desired solution functions how it was designed and as it was designed. By using a pilot, even in a small way, you can reduce your risk during implementation that something will not work as designed and end up causing issues, especially as you look to minimize the naysayers early and often throughout your launch. Trust me, they are out there.

Nail the key artifacts by keeping them simple and continue focusing on execution. The goal is to provide the vision of the future state and the precise roadmap to get there. Now is not the time to focus on the 72-page project document because that is how it always has been done.

When you want results, you need clear, concise documentation to support the path forward. Avoid the trap of busy work that will distract you from your goal.

As you have been communicating throughout the project, it is time to socialize the proposed solution. Communication is often the most overlooked part of the project. We know we need to keep senior leadership updated, but rarely spend enough time informing and building support from the grassroots level within the team itself as well as with teams that you interact with regularly. It is better to err on the side of over-communicating rather than under-communicating. You want to make sure that your benefits are not at the expense of someone else's team or their process. For a solution to truly be sustainable, stakeholders should be engaged early and often to ensure nothing is missed or result in unintended consequences.

Communication can truly make or break a project. As with other elements, it is easy to forget or to only focus on one aspect of communication. Set yourself up for success and minimize your chance of surprises down the road, communicate and influence cross-functionally as you go. Leave nothing to chance.

As we continue our journey toward execution, let's talk about everyone's favorite update medium...the status report. We are going to reboot the traditional wasted effort and make it useful in conveying the project message, progress and next steps.

Measuring success – status reports that demonstrate progress rather than colors

It should go without saying that the goal of any project is to achieve results for a particular business or team. Those desired outcomes are established during initiation and planning and are measured throughout the course of the project. As you may have guessed or experienced firsthand, communication is absolutely key throughout the project lifecycle.

The generally accepted method of providing communication to sponsors, stakeholders and others in the organization is a status report. Typically, status reports are updated weekly, biweekly at the absolute minimum with the goal of providing high level information around project achievements, timeline, budget and obstacles. You want senior leadership and others to know where the project is from a health perspective, minimize surprises and proactively call for reinforcements when needed. In most cases, it is simply to provide information and to demonstrate your progress.

Throughout my career, I have seen many versions of status reports. Some with a ton of information and some with barely enough. As I have said many times, simple is effective and that is exactly what we are striving for here. We want to provide enough detail that stakeholders and senior leaders are mindful of the project status, but not so much detail that we drag them into the weeds with us. A good status update paints the picture of what has been accomplished, what is scheduled to be accomplished near term, overall project health along with any risks or impediments.

Project health is color coded as red, yellow or green (more about that in a minute). The other elements can be as simple as bullet points outlining the key accomplishments and next steps. Additionally, you will want to be specific with requests or needs for assistance. If you are getting resistance from a key resource or simply need some air cover, you must clearly articulate the need and a specific call to action for your audience. Do not assume they know the details. I have seen many project managers make that mistake and it usually doesn't end well with either schedule delays, budgetary impact or some combination of horrors.

Project status definitions – what do red, yellow, green mean and why it is ok to be yellow

There is no need to overcomplicate things to make them look harder than they really are. Remember, simple is the goal. Far too often, project teams get overly complex in their solutions and then wonder why the project failed.

When you think about project health, it generally falls in three main categories:

- Overall Project Status
- Budget / Financial Status
- Timeline / Completion Status

With that in mind, let's look at fundamental project status definitions:

Green: This should be the clearest, easiest to complete.

- On track
- On budget
- No issues or risks
- No changes to timeline
- No resource constraints

Yellow: When / if your project hits yellow status, it becomes a little murky. If you are unsure whether or not your project is yellow, it probably is. You are looking for some combination of the following:

- Budget is slightly off track
- Timeline is in jeopardy, but not off the rails
- Potential for resource issues, but nothing is confirmed yet
- Issues or identified risks with documented mitigation plans.
- Reached current budget / funding level and awaiting additional funding.

When a project is trending yellow, you will want to define how you plan to get it back on track. This plan of action must include the proposed steps, resources or action items including dates that will move the project back to green status.

Red: Any combination of the following, could be all or some of them.

- Off budget
- Severe resource constraints
- Unaddressed risks or impediments

- Severe schedule delays resulting in missed deadlines or milestones

It goes without saying that every project team wants to stay green throughout the project lifecycle. However, that is just not realistic. It could happen, but most likely will not. Clearly you want to avoid red if at all possible since red means you are either in the ditch or heading straight for it. That said, **it is ok to be yellow**. Be comfortable with yellow.

Yellow means that you have identified issues or risks and found ways to avoid them. Yellow means that you realize your funding is reaching the end and you need the next draw from investment council. Yellow is ok. Understanding the path out of yellow rather than hiding it or making excuses is what separates successful projects (focused on execution) from failed projects.

Think back to the last project you led or a project team that you were a part of at some point. As you take the trip down memory lane, ask yourself a few questions…

1. Was the project truly successful and impactful to the business?
2. Were we busy executing or just busy?
3. Were we able to keep the project team and leadership engaged in the results or did they lose interest?

The answer to the second and third questions is usually the most telling. Most project teams are so bogged down in administrative nonsense that they appear busy but aren't really accomplishing much more than status updates and pretty dashboards. That is not to discount the importance of regular updates and tracking progress, but rather an observation of what usually derails successful projects.

There will be points where you do not have the all the answers and that you feel stuck. Everyone, including the most experienced project managers and senior leaders, feel that at times. It is at those moments that you realize you don't know what you need to know until you need it. The first step to getting over this hurdle is to realize that is part of the process and it is far more important to know where to get the right information than to be the sole source of information. The second step is, well, go get the information. Use it and move on.

To close out this chapter, I want to remind you that being busy is not enough. Everyone is busy. Everyone has excuses about why things cannot get done. However, busy is not execution. Execution is getting things done and adding value as a result of the project goals being accomplished. Use your project as a means to add value to your team, department or business. Stop being busy. If it isn't adding value, stop doing it and ask why am I doing this? The act of being busy can be disguised in many ways, but the most prevalent is also a trap. The trap of administrative excellence.

The trap of administrative excellence

"Strategy without tactics is the slowest route to victory, tactics without strategy is the noise before defeat."

— Sun Tzu

And now a few words about our nemesis...Administrative Excellence. Administrative Excellence is the super villain threatening to derail your project. It will destroy your ability to improve your team. It will limit your effectiveness in growing your business. It will restrict your ability to think from a customer's perspective.

Simply put, Administrative Excellence focuses on making the administrative tasks of a project eye catching, but there is no real substance behind them. It creates the illusion of execution. It is a focus on busy work that doesn't add any true value or bring the project any closer to delivering real results.

It is a killer pure and simple.

It will kill your project and limit your effectiveness.

It will destroy your productivity and limit any chance you have for making a difference.

Think about how many times these phrases have been used to describe a previous process change or project. I am sure these are examples that you are all too familiar with…

> *"We were hoping to see improvement over last year's results. Instead, we saw declines in many of the success factors we track".*
>
> *"We thought that productivity would increase, but nothing seems to have changed".*

"Why has employee satisfaction dipped again"?

"The percentage of projects meeting their business case objectives took a significant dip and we may have to explore cuts".

So, what do these data points tell us?

We have all seen projects deemed to be successful by the traditional PM criteria but fail to achieve the expected business results, or worse yet, have an adverse impact on the business.

No one sets out to do a bad job. We all go to work wanting to do our best and wanting to have a positive impact on our organizations. Many factors contribute to project failure – it is a complex challenge – but we have seen a few issues over and over again that no amount of project management will fix:

1. The right people are not involved – decisions being made by people who do not understand the underlying process connected to the decision, nor the potential impact of each of the options.

2. Project management measurements and rewards aligned with "on-time, on-budget" rather than return on investment (ROI).
3. Poor communication within the project team and between the team and the stakeholders.
4. Teams are required to adhere to processes that do not fit the problem they are trying to solve. This could be in the form of "check the box" templates for project reviews with no one understanding why the requirement for the template exits.

People have forgotten what execution looks like, so in lieu of true results, they demand the illusion of execution from their project teams, requiring project managers to treat the symptoms instead of treating the disease. As a result, PMs dutifully create the charters with the milestones, list the deliverables and schedule team meetings. PMOs hold project reviews and go through the PowerPoint decks with the red, yellow, and green status boxes and the action plan bullets. From the outside, it looks like a well-run system. But what we are really seeing is simply the illusion of execution as the team collectively falls into "the trap of administrative excellence." It looks good - the status boxes are all green, the paperwork is all there and the PMO is happy. No one would blame anyone for not taking any action.

There is no apparent reason to change anything. Until there is.

It's time to take a different approach. It is time to break the cycle and start getting things done. Think about a time when you experienced first-hand a well-run, successful project where the initiative delivered on all of the primary objectives, engaged the right people and make continual progress despite setbacks and competing priorities. Go ahead, pause a minute to think about that. I'll wait. If you've experienced a well-run project, chances are it left an impression on you.

Breaking free from the trap:

1. Bolting on the latest change management tools and theories to your project delivery methodology will not solve this problem.
2. Hiring a consultant will not fix this – Leadership cannot be delegated to a third party.
3. You cannot have accountability without empowerment, as long as you control the "how" you kill any sense of ownership, and you absolve your people from all accountability.
4. Stop checking boxes – empower and engage employees on the project team and especially those closest to the customer and the process to develop solutions.
5. Hold leadership and project teams accountable for delivering tangible, real results and progress – Not just status reports and pretty colors that everyone forgets as soon as the project closes.

Depending on your organization and culture, these changes may be easier said than done. However, even the smallest improvements can make a difference and it is rare to change minds overnight, but let your results begin to shift the corporate frame of reference.

Remember the secret sauce to effectiveness is all about execution and not just pretty reports and "keeping people in the loop". Yes, senior leaders and stakeholders have to be informed, but not at the expense of execution. Status reports should be simple and reflect what is getting accomplished, what needs to be done and what risks or impediments exist.

Project teams spend too much time on status updates for senior leadership and not enough time on pure execution. Focus your limited time on what truly matters. Make senior leadership happy and deliver sustainable results.

Now that you know who the enemy is, you can defeat it.

Closing the project

"If you don't know where you are going, you'll end up someplace else."

- Yogi Berra

Thanks to your diligent focus on execution, building strong organizational support and aligning the right resources, you are ready to deliver a real solution. Notice I didn't say anything about it being final. While you may officially close a project by delivering on the promised deliverables; the process seeking continuous improvement should truly never end. That is because there is no finish line. Nothing is ever final. It is an iterative process where you will look to continue to measure, refine and improve.

A focus on continuous improvement allows you to build a sustainable solution because you know it will need to change over time. Companies and processes are no different than people. You will either get better or worse; but will never stay the same. Those that realize this fact become relentless in their pursuit of improvement and those that don't fall by the wayside. If someone is pushing you for the "final" result, you may be in a no-win situation. According to a McKinsey & Company study in 2016, that type of narrow viewpoint is far too common and one of the main reasons why 70% of process changes fail or are sub-optimal once implemented. You may need to adjust how you frame the discussion, but always remember that "final" is a somewhat arbitrary term.

As you prepare to close out your project, there are a handful of deliverables that you will want to produce and track:

1. **Future state metrics and key performance indicators**: This is how you will not only measure success, but also how you will track continuing improvements and adjustments.
2. **Project Summary Report**: Summarize results from testing, pilot and early stage measurements. Proactively identify areas where adjustments may need to occur near term. (Don't let anyone fool you, no project is perfect. Despite the theories, reality is that there may be elements that are not completely in line with project goals and may require adjustment).
3. **Comparison to Original State**: Summarize the future state benefits and projected improvement based on the original business case, metrics and data. What led you to begin the project and why is this result better than what you had?

If your project is ready for close, ideally you have achieved your objectives, added value to the business and improved your process or functional team. The project is a done and everyone is ready to get back to business as usual. One less thing on the to-do list.

However, contrary to popular belief, if you go beyond the project close, you can achieve a greater impact and a greater benefit over time. If you believe in continuous improvement and refinement, then you know the project never truly ends. It only shifts from a project focus to business as usual.

Unfortunately, most project managers and businesses do not maintain this mindset. The project closes and everyone moves on to either the next item on the list or the next fire drill. This is exactly the mindset that will kill process improvements long term. When the process breaks down or deadlines loom, people tend to revert back to what they are comfortable with rather than what was implemented. Once this happens, there is no path back. You most likely lose the progress you made through the project and will end up starting over at some point under a new project wasting even more money than the first time.

The sad reality is that far too many businesses and teams operate this way. This behavior leads to wasted effort, wasted time and wasted money. On top of all that, it leads to lower morale and poor views of leadership. Nothing is worse than for a team to feel as if they wasted their time. We have all felt that at some point in our careers as the result of a half-assed project or poor implementation and it didn't feel great. Don't do that. Remember how you felt and how the team felt when they felt their effort was wasted. That has been the script for far too many projects in far too many companies.

Stop following the script, in fact ignore it altogether. As of this moment, commit to breaking the cycle of ineffective change. Instead of the usual way of doing things, focus on execution and continuous improvement.

Be the change your organization needs.

Be the change you want to see.

Be the change you always wanted to create.

Project management simplified

"If you can't explain it to a six-year old, you don't understand it yourself."

- Albert Einstein

People underestimate simple often to their own disadvantage. How many times have you encountered a person who liked an idea, but then made a comment that it was too simple? In some cases, it is definitely warranted, but when it comes to process changes and implementation, simple is not necessarily a bad thing. We have all seen good ideas cast aside because they seem too "simple" to work.

Throughout my career, I have found a few truths that are synonymous with effective solutions. First and foremost, the solution was simple which in turn reduced the learning curve around implementation and monitoring. I know, I know, you are tired of hearing about simple, but trust me you will face all kinds of resistance when it comes to effective execution.

Simple is not sexy, it is practical.

Simple is not limited to business today, it is scalable for the future.

Simple is not wasted effort, it is sustainable.

Simple saves careers. Enough said.

Simple can save money and improve customer service.

Second, a simple process doesn't rely on an overly complicated workflow or multiple handoffs. It allows for creativity and empowerment which, when done within reason, can have a dramatic impact on employee morale and customer experience. People feel like they are owners and as such transform into caretakers of "their" process rather than hired hands who work for some faceless company. With this ownership mentality, customer experience improves because they are dealing with the "owners" rather than some drone just passing time between lunch and quitting time.

Another benefit of simple is that you can modify as needed with relative ease. You will not need to rip everything down to the studs every single time you want to make a modification. If something doesn't work as intended, fix it. Change it based on what you learn from your metrics or on feedback from those closest to the new process. Do what needs to be done based on the data you are receiving from your customers, employees or both. Continuous improvement is just that...continuous. Always strive to find better, faster, smarter ways to do things. Look for metrics that go beyond the bottom line and translate into far more lasting measures of success like employee retention, customer pull through rate and retention. These are the true measures of success long term.

Finally, when we think of simple, the philosophy should apply to the tools used in managing a project as well as the process created. Chapter Ten will provide some ideas for creating your own simplified templates that can be used throughout the lifecycle of a project. Whether it is launching a new initiative, closing a project or providing a status update, you are covered. This is an end to end methodology that can help you manage a project from initiation to close in a clear concise manner.

Additionally, you will find that the templates definitely follow the simple theme, but also allow for a degree of customization. I think you will find that once you get beyond one or two pages of anything, it loses its impact. If you do encounter that, pause for a moment and ask yourself if the additional information is really adding value or if it is just filling whitespace. If the latter is your reason, you are caught in administrative excellence my friend and you need to get away from it immediately.

With all projects and initiatives, the primary goal should be to add value to the organization. Focus on one simple question when creating your project artifacts:

Does this content or document add value to the organization, or does it merely check a box?

If you answer that question honestly every time, you will be focused on adding value and executing on your project rather than creating content for the sake of content. Make no mistake about it, this is not common thinking. Given the state of project failures in most companies, focusing on value-add activities is not the rule of the day.

At the time of this writing, we are mired in a professional culture of box checking and administrative excellence. It is time for a revolution. It is time for a change. It is a time to forget the old, ineffective way of doing things and build a new future.

Join the revolution. Lead by example using simple and effective project management delivering end to end solutions. Add value and focus on execution. If you take the opportunity to look at the big picture and how all the pieces connect, you will start seeing what is coming around the corner and then begin driving sustainable change for your organization, your community and quite possibly the world.

Are you ready to break free from the status quo and join the revolution? If you have read this far, I think you are ready indeed.

Simplified toolkit

Now let's look at the tools and templates that will become the basic artifacts for your project. This is the foundation of your toolkit. It is something that can be built and refined over time, but like any survival kit, you want to have the basics. All of these tools are customizable to your needs, but I wanted to make sure you had the fundamentals outlined as a template of sorts to get you going. Regardless of the format used, make sure your project templates are simple, easy to use and add value to the initiative.

Here are the artifacts that we will walk through:

a. Project Proposal
b. Project Charter
c. Resource Needs
d. Stakeholder Identification & Analysis
e. Communication Plan
f. Project Kickoff Checklist
g. Risk Tracker
h. Status Report

Project proposal

At initiation, you will want to explore whether or not a project is viable or even needed before embarking on a costly journey. A project proposal accomplishes this by defining the problem you are trying to solve, how you can solve it and what happens if you do nothing to solve it. The proposal should include the following:

1. Project Name
2. Project Goal(s)
3. Definition of the problem / opportunity (will form the basis of your problem statement later)
4. Proposed Solution(s)
5. Resources Needed
6. Interdependencies (if any)
7. Scope
8. Projected Benefits
9. Potential Risks of Inaction
10. Projected Schedule

Project Charter

A charter should simply and succinctly define the problem, measures of success, deliverables and scope. If more details help you plan, so be it. However, don't let it paralyze you into overanalyzing the situation. Either there is a problem or there isn't. Will this project get you to the solution?

Here are the key elements you need to include:

- A. Project Summary
- B. Problem Statement
- C. Project Deliverables
- D. Scope
- E. Resources Needed
- F. Key Milestones
- G. Measures of Success

Resource Needs

You need to define the resources that you need throughout the project, the level of their involvement (i.e. time commitment and the expertise you need). From there, confirm availability and assign tasks. An important aspect that is almost always overlooked is providing a reason behind why you need their expertise and what happens if you cannot get it. This may come in handy later on as you are trying to influence the decision makers in providing the needed resources.

1. **Name:** who is the person you need for the project?
2. **Role:** what role will they play on the project team?
3. **Function:** what group will they represent?
4. **Time Commitment:** how much will you need them? Think in terms of number of hours per week rather than percentage.
5. **Rate (if applicable):** if the resource is external or if the hours will be assessed back to the

project (generally IT work falls into this category)

6. **Expertise:** what does this person bring to the project and why are they critical for success? Think about what would happen if you didn't have their expertise.

Stakeholder Identification & Analysis

If you understand the stakeholders that are impacted by your project, you can not only tailor your communication to their needs but align deliverables to positively impact their teams. A successful project doesn't just shift work around, but rather it finds a solution to streamline a process allowing everyone to benefit.

Know your stakeholders. Know their pain points and then position your project as the solution. Here is what you will want to include in your Stakeholder Analysis:

A. Stakeholder name / function
B. Key challenges (if known)
C. Support project?
D. Determine the role of each stakeholder. This includes, but not limited to: sponsor, resource, customer or decision maker / approver. Remember a customer is not just the end user or external to the company. A customer is anyone who is impacted by your project.

E. Link to communication plan to align communication needs with expectations.

Communication Plan
  Understand what information people want or need, how they want to receive it and how often they need it. Once you know all of that, assign someone to own communication. Be mindful of the medium that you use and do not rely solely on email. If you want to keep something a secret, send an email. And one last thing...

Communicate, Communicate, Communicate (early and often)

  Be sure to include the following:

  A. Stakeholder Name
  B. Information they need
  C. Frequency of Communication
  D. Medium to be used
  E. Communication Owner

Risk Assessment

All projects have risks and virtually all risks can be addressed if you know about them. Conduct a risk assessment to know where you stand periodically through the project and minimize surprises (the bad kind).

It is not enough to merely identify a risk. You need to determine the likelihood of it occurring and the impact it will have if it occurs. Additionally, you will need to outline a mitigation plan and an owner so that in the unlikely event a problem does occur, you are ready to take action. When constructing your risk assessment, you will need to include the following:

A. Risk Name
B. Description
C. Severity
D. Probability of Occurrence
E. Mitigation Plan
F. Owner

Project Kickoff Checklist

By focusing on your preparation early in the project, you increase your chances of improved support and buy-in from the start. If you have a productive project kick-off, you increase your chances of early engagement by the project team and improve clarity around the project goals / deliverables.

Sample Kickoff Checklist
Pre-Launch Engagement

- The project goals have been clearly established
- Project deliverables and goals have been reviewed with and approved by the Project Sponsor
- The project team has been briefed on the initiative and understands why they were selected to participate
- Key resources and suppliers understand their impact and their roles in the project
- Functional managers who supply project resources have been briefed and have committed the necessary resources for project completion
- Create a project site or folder (via SharePoint, DropBox, Shared Drive or another collaborative tool)
- Load required tools and templates into collaboration tool

Project Details

- Project plan has been established

- Specific tasks and responsibilities are been clearly defined (who is going to do what and when)
- There is a clearly defined change management process in place
- Communication plan has been defined and instituted – including frequency of status reports
- Operating mechanisms (i.e. project team meetings, stakeholder meetings and senior level updates, etc.) have been scheduled
- Define established ground rules for working sessions and team meetings
- Define & document the accepted process for change requests, risk identification and task completion
- Confirm all required templates are available on project site

Project Launch
- Review project charter, deliverables, objectives and communication plan with project team

- Provide overview of project timeline along with key milestones
- Outline any dependencies and ensure team is mindful of critical path tasks
- Commit to open and honest dialogue with the project team – be sincere and follow through on that
- Review upcoming meetings and near-term deliverables
- Answer questions – clarity can help drive execution

Status Report

From stakeholders to sponsors, everyone will want to know if the project is making progress or stuck in the mud. From the beginning, define the frequency of status updates and then be consistent. This will help to not only raise awareness of your good work, but also to draw attention to potential risks and impediments before they become a problem. Be sure to highlight milestones achieved or quick wins to increase the success chatter around your project.

Your status report should include the following elements:

1. Project Overview Section
    a. Date of Report
    b. Project Name
    c. Project Summary
    d. Project Manager Name
    e. Sponsor(s)
2. Project Health Section
    a. Budget Health (Red, Yellow or Green)
    b. Schedule Health (Red, Yellow or Green)

      c. Overall Health (Red, Yellow or Green)
3. Project Update
    a. Major Accomplishments since last update
    b. Upcoming Deliverables & Milestones
4. Issue / Risk Identification
    a. Identified Issues
    b. Potential Impact
    c. Owner
5. Summary of Changes (if applicable)
    a. Change Description
    b. Type (Scope, Budget, Schedule, etc.)
    c. Approver

Putting it all together

"We are all faced with a series of great opportunities brilliantly disguised as impossible situations."

- Charles Swindoll

Hopefully at this point you see that project management does not have to be a complex mess. It can be simplified and focused through initiation, planning, execution, implementation, and beyond. Most projects are led by someone who is not a project manager by trade. With limited resources for non-technology projects, it can be difficult to focus on execution while you are focusing on your full-time, regular job and trying to progress on the project at the same time. At some point, whether a quarter end, year-end or just the regularly unscheduled fire drill, priorities can shift and before you know it your project is now number fifteen on the top ten list of things to do.

Regardless of your industry, leading effective projects comes down to execution. All of the other noise will get in the way if you let it. In some cases, the perceived noise might be unavoidable or even legitimate, but it can and must be minimized. If you are able to do that while delivering on project objectives, you will succeed. If something takes priority for a time, let it. Things happen, life happens. Like anything else, try to work on the project or at least review your deliverables a few times a week, even if only for fifteen minutes. It may sound silly, but when that deadline passes, you will find it easier to return to your project and continue.

If an organization is ineffective at leading sustainable change, you will start to see an impact in the areas of customer retention and revenue. To drive sustainable change, your mindset must evolve beyond project management and become more about change management. Look at the big picture and see beyond the project close for additional opportunities. It doesn't need to be a formal project, but you do need to have the right people engaged. As you continuously improve your process, continue to mentor and grow the skillset of your team. If they can follow your example, they will learn new skills and provide bench strength which in turn provides increased capacity for change.

Be innovative and relentless in your pursuit of change that adds value to the organization rather than change for the sake of change. Continually foster cross-functional relationships for collaboration beyond your project. The end of the project is just the start of the next phase of continuous improvement. If you continue to refine the process over time and leverage metrics to track progress, you will know where to focus your efforts going forward. Rely on the smart people within your team and organization that are your customers to provide feedback on areas of improvement. It is the best data you will ever collect.

Remember that simplicity is the key to success. Projects and process changes today are mired in bureaucracy and poor execution. As you embark on your next initiative, think about incorporating a few small changes:

1. Delegate to and empower team and project resources
2. Build strong, yet small project teams
3. Become nimble, even if your organization isn't - Flexibility and empowerment to make changes as you go or as warranted by discoveries during the project
4. Minimal status reporting – report regularly but keep it focused on the objectives, what was accomplished and what is coming next.

Build.

Measure.

Learn.

Refine.

The process should never end. Remember, processes are like people, they either get better or worse over time, but never stay the same. Strive to take small, incremental steps to become better every day. Change doesn't need to happen all at once to be impactful. Learn from the data you track, don't just put it on a PowerPoint slide and send it off to your boss. Allow your team to make process adjustments as needed to build a culture that embraces change.

As you move forward, remember the following things. First, add value every day. Second, focus on execution not administrative excellence. Third, shift away from the current trend of ineffective change management. Finally, it is never too late to embrace new ideas. This is a revolution against mediocre change and ineffective projects. It is about empowering people and improving customer experience beyond the normal standards.

Join the revolution.

Now that we have gotten this far, let's move on to Part 2 and go beyond methodology and concept to practical application.

PART II

Theory and ideas are great, but they must be applied and used to add any value. Without a roadmap, how do you know if you are on the right track or tackling things that matter? This section attempts to dive deeper into the concepts from the first half of the book with an opportunity for practical application to a current or previous project. It provides a guide and a frame of reference to operationalize the concepts from the first half to increase the odds of success. This is not meant to solve every imaginable problem, but to get you thinking about how to apply concepts and see a path forward for your own projects and process changes. There is a lot to learn from past projects, failures and theories.

When companies look for ways to grow their business, add value or increase market share, they tend to compete on the same things. If you look beyond product, price and other typical measures, you will find something just under the surface that can add tremendous value, increase market share and improve customer loyalty. Typically, it is one of the last things companies look at when they develop a growth strategy, but it is there. It just needs to be unlocked.

Process can be a strategic asset just like technology, money or information.

Process can be a competitive weapon to increase revenue and retain customers.

Process is underappreciated and often ignored (unless it is flawed).

Process is the way things get done every day.

This is the lifeblood of your business. It is the way to build a thriving business, support your customers dynamically and add continual value to shareholders. Business process optimization is not built around technology innovation or enhancements per se, but rather value innovation. Find ways to create or enhance value to your customers and learn from your non-customers and competitors. Don't be afraid to look beyond your current industry to find great, scalable ideas and better ways of doing things. Just because an idea came from the banking world doesn't mean it couldn't apply in healthcare.

By optimizing your business processes, especially those impacting your customer, you can create a key differentiator from the competition. Go beyond the normal ideas around value creation and start with the largest asset you own…the way you get things done.

Why focus on execution?

Execution Defined

The carrying out or putting into effect of a plan, order, or course of action.

Why does execution matter?

Execution is the fundamental component to any successful change initiative or project. As you have guessed by now, I am obsessed with execution. It is the key to everything good. Focus on the important things, simplify them, improve them and monitor them. Nothing happens without execution. The key question for most people is this...are you busy executing or just busy? If it is the latter, then your project will be in serious trouble long term.

You will not be able to solve every problem all at once. Far too many projects have grand charters and timelines but start to struggle when things do not go as planned or resources become unavailable. Change that mindset. Focus on results and small wins. Link your project to the overall strategy to ensure you are staying on the road and avoiding scope creep.

Execution is everything. Without it, nothing sustainable can be created and processes cannot successfully change.

Linking strategy to execution

In short, to make any change, regardless of size and scope, you must be able to execute. If it is a personal change, you must be committed every day to making the change through small, incremental improvements. If a business setting, you need to build trust and commitment on a larger scale. Far too often, strategic discussions are limited to the executive team or senior management and it rarely makes it to the team that actually does the work. That is a critical miss in planning as well as a missed opportunity. Of course, this doesn't mean that you should broadcast every strategic decision or planning session to all levels of the organization. Rather, it means that you should build execution into your strategy and execution involves the people who are tasked with implementation and beyond. It means going beyond your executive committee and engaging your teams at all levels of the organization, but especially those impacted by the strategy.

Through engagement you can lay the groundwork for ownership. Inspire your team with the strategic vision. Inspire them to feel a part of it and to add value to it. To minimize the risk of distrust or lack of enthusiasm, engage your people on the front lines, those who must execute the strategy every day. They are the ones with the process expertise and are also able to troubleshoot with customers. If they are removed from the process or unknown variables are ignored (you don't know what you don't know) that impact the day-to-day operations, the strategy will be ineffective because it lacks the linkage to how things really operate. This is the linkage that the team working in and with the process can provide.

Through this kind of engagement, you will link your team to the solution and thus fulfill a basic human need for recognition. This allows your team to feel a part of the strategy, to own it and make it succeed. This is also how you create trust, commitment and cooperation long after the strategy is in place. You team should not be measured by their hierarchical value, but rather by the value that they contribute to the organization.

How speed can trump perfection (sometimes)

Speed combined with hard work can trump almost anything. By focusing on speed, you are indirectly focusing on execution. Perfection is paralysis. If you wait for perfection, nothing will get accomplished. You will be standing still while your competition is running circles around you.

Be fast, deliver value to your clients every day. The big goals take time, but the day to day execution relies on speed not perfection. Take the time to build a simple, scalable process but don't focus solely on perfection. Set yourself and your business up with a plan and then begin executing as soon as possible.

Strategy can be slow, but execution must be fast.

Execution should add value, be relentless in your pursuit of value creation. Don't waste time focusing on perfection at the expense of execution.

Execution drives your organization forward. To accomplish your goals, you will need speed.

Reflection

How could a focus on execution help your project, organization, prioritization, etc.? How has a failure to focus on execution or plan for execution negatively impacted your team or organization?

Focusing on the right things

Simple applies to the framework that you use to manage your project just as much as it applies to the outcome of the project itself. You want to drive consistent results when designing a new process, aligning resources or reengineering an existing process. In order to solve for the future, you need to first understand where you are today. If you do not know how a process works today or the current risks associated with current state, how on earth can you expect to improve it?

The methodology below has been developed through years of research and practical use to create lasting, sustainable change within teams and organizations. It begins with a candid assessment of the current state process, environment, technology, resources, etc. Based on that assessment, you can begin the design for a future state that builds upon what is working well, fixes what is not working today while identifying the tools and resources needed for tomorrow. It is ok to think beyond your current initiative and plan for the future; just be mindful of your current capabilities and limitations before committing to big changes.

To be effective over the course of a project, the team needs to revisit deliverables and ensure there are toll-gates at each stage so that you can validate if you are on the right track or heading for the ditch. This serves two purposes. First it keeps you focused on the right deliverables. Just because you defined something initially doesn't mean that hypothesis could not change through discovery. It is always easier to course correct during a project than post implementation. Really, there is no difference with technical project in that regard. Second, it provides a pulse check so you can ensure that everything was captured and documented appropriately and clearly. If not, a tollgate allows you the opportunity to get the documentation right but also to get the perspective of an independent third party, like a project governance team or a steering committee. Sometimes when you are so close to a process, it is hard to see the disconnects because your brain starts filling in the gaps for you.

Communication is critical. In fact, it may be the most critical component next to execution. You want buy-in first from the stakeholders and then from the Sponsor. Build the coalition as you develop the project charter and you will go a long way to getting the resources and support you need to execute. Additionally, this serves to increase buy-in, resource allocation and potentially even funding long term.

Importance of Simple – why simple works?

Simple works on many levels. Unfortunately, it is often taken only at face value and easily dismissed as limited. That is a form of resistance thanks to the idea that complex problems have complex solutions which has been used since the nineties. Simple can apply regardless of your process or industry is a demonstrated game changer with respect to customer interaction and risk management.

Simple processes do not have an overly complex workflow, nor do they have endless loops of unneeded handoffs that add minimal (if any) value. It focuses on empowerment and making the people who use the process the owners of the process. As owners, you can influence and change the mindset of your team and create a greater customer focus while allowing for a compliant, yet dynamic solution that becomes scalable over time.

Measuring success

How do you measure success in a project or within a business? Far too often managers and businesses get caught in the web of a cost/benefit analysis (CBA) that is a typical project artifact. I would argue that the true value of a project goes beyond a CBA. By building a new process or refining an existing one, you may not see a direct impact to sales or a cost reduction. So, if that is the case, how can you measure results?

Look beyond the traditional measures of success. The impact of your process changes may be felt far beyond growth for this quarter or year. If done correctly and continuously improved, you can lay the foundation for the future. Think about that for a moment. Stop thinking in terms of the here and now but look beyond.

Here are some considerations for measuring success when you think past cost reduction, efficiency and increased volume:

- Think about the impact if you simplify a process and improve employee retention.
- Think about what empowering employees could do for your organization and customer experience.
- Think about how a simpler process could improve customer experience and drive increased volume long term.

Stop playing the short game and start playing the strategic game. The strategic game adds value beyond this month or this quarter and instead builds the future of growth for years to come. It will improve a process in the near term, but It is not limited to a quick win. Rather it should build recurring value over time if done correctly. Process and strategy must be just as dynamic as the business environment.

Reflection Point

How could a simple process benefit your team or organization? How could you build measurements that actually represent what you do rather than legacy metrics that have always been there?

Influencing change Part 1

Influencing is the absolute lifeblood of an accidental project manager. More often than not, you need to accomplish something that requires buy-in from other process owners or stakeholders or even potentially people who just don't want to change. (gasp...how could that be??). Regardless of the reason, influencing plays a critical role in getting things done, especially when you don't own the resources doing the actual work.

Most people go about influencing the absolute wrong way. In my experience, I have seen people try one of two tactics. Either they take a hardline stance and overstate their position, or they are too passive and give up more than they get. Regardless of the tactic, most people fail to achieve their goal.

As an accidental project manager, you need to be able to bring people together under a common goal. This can be especially difficult when the resources you need do not report to you. That is why it is so important to align your initiative with organizational needs, especially if there is a cross-functional impact. Building up influencing skills takes time, but once you have your coalition, it is much easier to move the big rocks and get the needed resources. Influencing skills will play a huge role throughout your project. It is a critical skill to get anything done. As I mentioned earlier, cross-functional stakeholders DO NOT care about your charter, process maps or project artifacts. They DO care about process simplification, improving resource capacity, expense reduction and growing revenue. If you can link your deliverables to these types of goals, your path to building a strong coalition becomes much easier.

It isn't about merely "convincing" someone that you are right. It is about getting them to see the benefits of the change from their perspective. The best way to do that is to frame the discussion from the perspective of your stakeholder. Understand how a potential change may impact another team and proactively look to address potential issues or imperfections in the proposed changes. By doing that, you are deflecting any potential ammunition they may use to derail your project. You are proactively telling them that there may be short term pain and acknowledging what it is in specific terms.

If you don't fully understand their process, now is the perfect time to learn it. You do not have to understand every detail but do you best to gain a high-level understanding. This will not only benefit the project but will instantly improve your credibility as a leader. Additionally, it will go a long way in short-cutting the approval time because you are already aligning your "customers".

If someone is particularly change resistant, taking time to understand their perspective is a must do. To be successful, it is a non-negotiable step. You need to understand the source of their resistance and get them to see why the change is necessary. Most importantly you want to demonstrate how the change will actually benefit them. Too often we assume that the other person's views are in conflict with our own, but that is not always the case. We just need to take the time to see things from their point of view.

While this is easier said than done, there are some techniques that can help accomplish this. To go in guns blazing and aggressively state your position is definitely not the way to go. In fact, even if your position is correct, you will most likely encounter significant resistance with this approach. It is far better to ask clarifying questions that focus on the "what" and the "how". These are questions that cannot be answered with a yes or no but require some thought. Plus, by asking a "how" question, you engage the other person to help find a solution to the shared problem or to meet the shared goal. If you can avoid a simple yes or no question, you get the other person, team, whatever to contribute to the discussion. It virtually eliminates the opportunity for a quick no and not much else from a dialogue perspective.

This is not necessarily something we all have experience doing. In his book, *Never Split the Difference*, former FBI negotiator Chris Voss talks about using calibrated questions to engage the other person and asking them for help. This not only creates an atmosphere of cooperation, but it also gives the other person the opportunity to speak about things that are critical to them and will reveal important information as a result. He recommends calibrating questions that encourage another person to focus on a solution rather than pure resistance.

It is absolutely critical to make sure that your benefits are not at the expense of someone else's team or their process. For a solution to truly be sustainable, stakeholders should be engaged early and often to ensure nothing is missed or result in unintended consequences. If it is clear that your changes will negatively impact another part of the organization, resistance will settle in and your changes will be dead on arrival. Ask calibrated questions to gain a better understanding of shared priorities and identify specific needs of their team or process.

Not all change can or will be successful. We can try every trick in the book, but sometimes there are fundamental problems that are too much to overcome. As an accidental project manager, you want to be aware of things going sideways before you go too far. It is much easier to course correct while you are still building the solution than after you deploy it. That said there is always an element of continuous improvement that should be expected.

With that in mind, there are several common sources of failure to be mindful of as you approach the project:

1. Trying to take shortcuts – organizations must wholly commit to making a change in order to deliver results.
2. Unable or unwilling to involve employees, especially front-line employees – if the team feels like they own it, they will make it happen
3. Sending conflicting messages or none at all – clear, consistent communication is key to achieving goals
4. Senior management not walking the talk – leaders should be modeling the desired mindset and behavior, relentlessly pursuing execution
5. Lacking clarity of vision – clear vision provides an anchor for the overall strategy
6. Unrealistic expectations – if expectations are unrealistic, the project is set to fail from the start

Any and all of the above sources of failure can derail a project at any time. While not all of them are within your control, you can reduce the impact of most of them through effective communication at all levels of the organization. Don't just preach to the choir because it is easier. Seek out people that have a different frame of reference or a different level of experience and get them to poke holes in the concept or idea. Set yourself up for success and minimize your chance of surprises down the road, communicate and influence cross-functionally as you go. Leave nothing to chance.

That said, communication can only get you so far. It is absolutely critical that senior leadership walks the talk early and often. Without clarity of vision, support and actions that reinforce the change, all the meetings in the world will not save the project.

The sad reality is that far too many businesses and teams do not operate this way. As a result, they experience wasted effort, wasted time and wasted money rather than results. On top of all that, repeated project failures lead to lower morale and poor views of leadership. Nothing is worse than for a team to feel as if they wasted their time. We have all felt that at some point in our careers as the result of a half-assed project or poor implementation and it didn't feel great. Don't do that. Remember how you felt and how the team felt when they felt their effort was wasted. That has been the script for far too many projects in far too many companies.

Reflection Point

Think back to a project or initiative where you had to influence a stakeholder, decision maker or process owner. What did you do? Were you successful? How could you improve in the future?

Influencing change Part 2

No one truly likes to change. Typically, people embrace it under one of two circumstances. First, when it aligns to something that we need or want more, something beyond the status quo. It must link to or provide a path forward to more growth, productivity or revenue with less risk. There has to be some benefit to the other person. The other side of the coin is less pleasant. If change doesn't align with our present goals or needs, humans tend to embrace it when they have no other option. When it is the last best choice, it becomes a need.

The key to influencing change is to align the why behind the project to the needs of the impacted business teams or functions. They do not care about charters or project plans or schedules. They care about adding value, increasing income and productivity while decreasing risk. If you can connect the project why to the needs of those that you need to make it successful, you will win their support and in the end drive long lasting change.

Understand the roles that are impacted by your project and how that change will impact them. This is less about influencing and more about knowing your audience and targeting your efforts rather than treating everyone the same. That is how most people approach a political hurdle and then they wonder why it didn't work. To ensure you break down political barriers and build the right coalition, you need to know the following:

1. Who are my detractors?
2. Who will / could disrupt this project?
3. Who has the most to lose with a change to the status quo?
4. Who are my supporters?

5. Who will naturally align with this initiative and support it?
6. Who has the most to gain as a result of this strategic change?

Identify your supporters and detractors. Ignore everyone in the middle at this point. Move quickly to communicate with your various groups and create a win-win scenario as best you can. Understand their perceived pain points and anticipate their objections. If you cannot bring resolution to their objections, isolate your detractors by building a broader coalition of support while addressing their key objections.

The key to winning over your detractors is to know their likely angles of attack early and build counterpoints supported by your coalition and backed by data and reason. Once you do that, you will reduce the risk of a political war before it even begins. This doesn't mean that all of a sudden everyone will agree with you, but you increase your chances of pressing forward with minimal resistance. It will never be perfect, but that shouldn't stop you from making your case, supporting it with data and logic to keep moving forward.

Reflection Point

Think of a previous or current project, how could you better align stakeholders, resistors and supporters to move toward a common goal? Looking back at a failed initiative, can you see where the influencing failed?

Typical Sticking Points

Why your initiative will not succeed?

There are several critical factors that need to be in place if you want to create sustainable change in your organization. This list is not all inclusive, but includes the must have items:

- Leadership buy-in and support of your initiative
- Resources aligned and engaged for the project
- Business case / the "why" behind the project is strong.

- *The team understands the reason(s) behind the change and are actively supporting the project.*

To be honest, there are definitely some that are more important than others on this list. If you have nothing but leadership support and effective resources engaged, you will be much further along the path to success than 80% of projects. That is why most of them fail. Now, look at your own organization and you own team. Pause for a moment and answer the following question honestly. When you think about the critical factors linked to your initiative, how many could you say are in place?

You do not have to hold out for perfect, sometimes good enough is, well, good enough. It is not about starting at the ideal state, but rather beginning the journey to the ideal state. Change initiatives should be time bound, but not to the extent that the deadline compromises the long-term benefits.

Resource constraints and why they don't matter

Typically projects over-estimate the quantity of resources or expertise needed, but often fail to get the right resource. It is not critical to get everyone in a particular department on every project and in every project meeting. It is critical to get the "right" people.

Best practices include:

1. Identify what resources you need, when you need them and why they are critical to the project
2. Stop meeting for the sake of having a meeting
3. Empower the team to execute on deliverables by the needed deadline – engage leadership to provide air cover or realign priorities (if needed)
4. Engage people as you need them and run it like a move set. Think about that...generally speaking the entire cast is not around for the entire shoot, but rather they participate as needed / when needed to accomplish their deliverables

Subject matter expertise and why that really does matter (to a degree)

Many projects begin with a goal in mind, at least at a high level. Unfortunately, far too many projects fail to get deep enough to understand what is really happening.

1. Involve the people that actually do the work – especially those that are highly experienced in the nuances of the deliverables
2. Document the manual processes and workarounds – this is where you kick over rocks and are actually able to improve cycle time, customer experience and employee productivity
3. Identify solutions to those previously identified manual processes and workarounds – *"how would you build this if you started from scratch?"*
4. Find out where the problem areas are from the people that know the process the best – those that do it every day

Managing through organizational hurdles and objections

Execution is critical to any successful project, process change or strategy. Unfortunately, many companies (and individuals) have difficulty translating thought or strategy into action. Most people, managers included, believe that change is steep and challenging. That is the experience most of us have with change, but it doesn't always have to be painful. It all begins with an awareness that something needs to change. To drive effectiveness and a focus on continuous improvement and execution, companies and individuals must abandon conventional wisdom to bring about results. It is time to flip conventional wisdom on its head.

Typically, there are several obstacles that must be overcome regardless of the level of change. First, we have all heard of the excuse of limited resources. With a large-scale change effort, it is generally assumed that increased resources are required to execute upon it. The reality is that you need the resources most qualified to lead or participate in the project. You do not need an increase in resources if you have the right people.

The second obstacle is linked to motivation. How do you motivate the key players within your organization to carry out the execution of a strategic initiative? To make an initiative meaningful to your team, you must be transparent and tell them exactly why a change is required. If you engage the key influencers in your organization, they can help drive the message to all levels. Additionally, they can help make it meaningful to the larger organization. It allows you to play to your strengths and engage your high performers in building a solution.

Finally, you need to successful influence and navigate through the political minefield of your organization. This begins with understanding who are your strongest supporters and detractors. Don't focus on the neutral parties at this point. The goal is to build a win-win outcome for both groups as much as possible. There is no perfect solution and not everyone will be completely happy. That is reality. Build as broad of a coalition as you can and in doing so anticipate the needs or objections of your detractors. Attempt to mitigate or minimize those objections as much as possible. Like any negotiation, all parties need to give a bit to make the best solution for everyone. That is the fundamental goal from this exercise. By engaging all parties, you can build on the strengths by addressing needs that may have been overlooked and thus producing a larger coalition of support long term.

Overcoming these obstacles is not easy, but when you do, you will not only change the direction of your project, but you will break free of the status quo and the trap of ineffective change management. All obstacles are not created equal despite the fact that most companies treat them as such. Focus your efforts on those obstacles that require great effort. Leverage your coalition and poke holes in your theories. This is an opportunity to get a real-life pulse check. Be sure to note the low hanging fruit but leave the minor stuff alone at this point.

Why leadership matters to get a project off the ground and eventually completed

Leadership can mean the difference between a successful project and another that is dead on arrival. There are many reasons why you want Senior Leadership to support your project or initiative, but that support goes beyond funding.

- By engaging your leadership team early, you can position the importance to the organization and drive or influence the priority level
- Senior leadership must understand the "why" behind the project and how it benefits them
- Resource constraints can and will occur – leadership support helps to mitigate this risk by making the project a priority
- Anticipate potential obstacles and what type of escalation or support would be needed to mitigate – yes, some basic scenario planning is critical to this step

Reflection Point

What organizational hurdles have derailed or threatened to derail your project? How did you address them? Do you feel you had the tools and support to do so?

Building high performing teams

The empowerment / accountability link

As part of a team, most people want to be empowered to make decisions and use the expertise that they brought when they joined a company. Of course, not everyone craves this type of authority, but generally speaking I think the majority of people would prefer it over being micro-managed. While empowerment sounds great and makes a terrific topic, few really emphasize the other side of empowerment. That side is, of course, accountability.

These two should go hand-in-hand, but how do you instill a culture of empowerment and continuous improvement while holding people accountable. It starts with a detailed strategy that is clearly communicated to all teams and then allowing those talented people to set their own goals and measures of success and then communicating those through regular updates and working sessions.

Empowerment = Accountability.

You can't have one without other if you truly want a culture of high performance.

Involve people in making a process better or improving customer experience. It will allow them to use the skills they possess, but also help them to feel like they are adding value beyond their daily tasks. Empower them to take risks and learn from mistakes. Build a successful team, business or process around your best people. By allowing people to make decisions, learn from mistakes and take ownership, you will find that most will not only rise to the occasion, but you will build a strong bench for future growth.

Playing to your strengths – get the right people engaged

Everyone on a project team can contribute something or else they wouldn't be there. However, it is not just about recruiting experts (more on that in a minute), it is about leveraging skills that people bring based on their education, experience, perspective or some combination to the team. Allow them to be creative and challenge the status quo. If you don't do that, you will end up with a Frankenstein monster version of your current process and as a result you will not bring the desired results. More than likely you will just get a new version of the same pain points.

Don't rely solely on experts - why a fresh perspective can trump expertise and lead to effective change

There is a reason why companies or teams that have successfully transformed their business bring in people from other teams or industries...it works. When you have spent 15 years working with the same process or with the same team, it is hard to bring a fresh perspective. That doesn't mean that it cannot happen, it is just not common because we all fear change on some level and rely heavily on comfort.

Engage people in the process – from discovery to design and beyond. Don't be fooled by experience alone. Obviously, you want / need to have qualified people working on the project and your team, but that shouldn't be the end all be all. The ability to create a high performing team has little to do with the combined experience of the individual but rather on the dynamic that you create within the team. More often than not, deep levels of experience will only get you so far. Like

Steve Jobs used to say, "it's more fun to be a pirate than join the navy." Build a team of pirates. That is the secret to high performing teams – find the right mix of experience, creativity and execution. That will help create the culture of accountability that you need for long term success, but also leverage diverse backgrounds to see things from an entirely new lens.

Reflection Point

Think of a successful project or high performing team that you were on. What made them successful? How could you replicate that success on your own team or in your project?

Risk identification & mitigation

Risk identification and remediation – why is this important and why it shouldn't be a "check the box" activity

      Understanding the risks that exist within your process can literally be the difference between a successful project and one that is thrown on the scrap heap. Take time to work cross-functionally with the project team and stakeholders to account for risks from all angles. Be sure to identify even the most unlikely risk. At this point, you are not vetting the legitimacy, but rather brainstorming potential risks and how they could impact your project in the event that they occur.

As you go through your risk brainstorming and assessment process, consider the following:

1. How can you and the team proactively identify risks as well as the ways to avoid them before they become a problem?
2. How do you communicate risks and making them relevant beyond the project team?
3. How do you engage stakeholders and other business partners in the process? This cannot be done in a vacuum.

Balancing worst case scenario with contingency planning.

Being mindful about what could happen is not the same as being prepared for it. Just like car insurance, you do not plan to be in an accident, but you are prepared just in case you are. Same thing with projects. By completing a scenario-based risk assessment, you position yourself to proactively address risks if/when they arise. Will you anticipate everything? Of course not. The goal is to plan based on your business environment and the risks in your industry while being mindful of issues that arose during previous or similar projects. Risk management is not a one-time event, but a dynamic recurring exercise that should be data-driven and responsive to organizational or regulatory changes.

Reflection Point

How can you make project risks relevant to your stakeholders and get them to buy into your solutions?

Modern change management

In most organizations today, there is plenty of talk about change management, but not much real change. Here are some sobering facts around the reality of the current state of change management:

1. Even though many companies undertake large scale change initiatives, almost 75% of employees don't actually change how they work.
2. Initiatives are based on out of the box, established change management principles like ADKAR, Six Sigma and others

3. Regardless of the model, there is one common failure – employees are led from the top down rather than empowered to make changes based on how processes actually work rather than on how others "think" it works
4. When the project ends, the team reverts back to the way they did things prior to the project

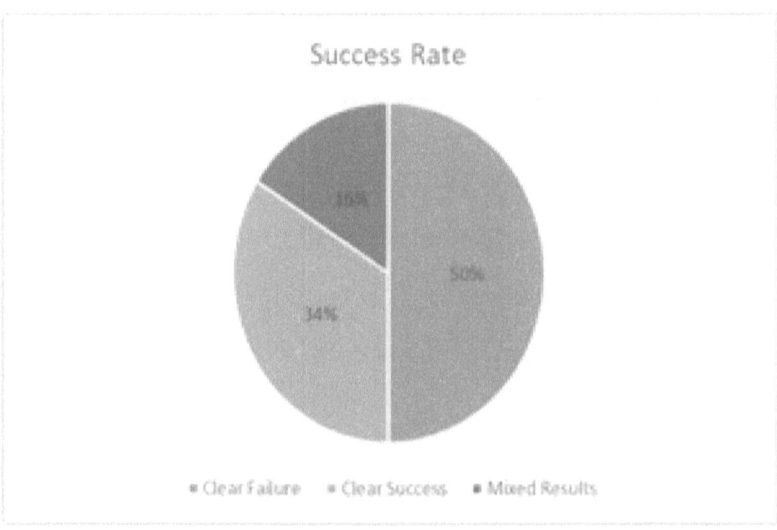

Source: Willis Towers Watson Study, 2013

Take a look at the graphic on the previous page - think about that data in the context of your own team or organization. How many scenarios are relatable? Probably more than most would care to admit. I know from my career I have experienced all of them at one time or another.

Let's face it, business, project management and process changes are far different today than they were five, ten or fifteen years ago. That said, change management must evolve as well. It cannot remain the same forever or aligned to a particular methodology because the organization got a good deal on training or because a Board Member read something about it in a magazine. Nothing against out of the box, established strategies, but change is not a one size fits all practice, nor is it linear (think ADKAR, Six Sigma, etc.). Every organization and team are different. Every process has slight nuances that need to be addressed specifically in the context of that process by people who know the process.

It cannot be only a solo or lone wolf effort (unless absolutely necessary). If leaders don't involve their teams, they cannot hope to expose the true root cause problems nor will they receive the benefit of fresh ideas and a sense of ownership from the people who know the process best. This improves morale, but also creates a strong competitive advantage for the long term through increased ownership and empowerment. I keep saying this and you are probably tired or reading it, but it is a fundamental truth to building a high performing process, team or business.

Modern business requires a forward-thinking approach to project / change management. To be effective long term and obtain the needed buy-in from your teams, it needs to be "open source". You are probably thinking, what does that mean? It means that rather than relying solely on top down directives and goals, organizations strive to build a culture of change and continuous improvement at all levels with a co-created strategy with the extended team that includes grassroots engagement, empowerment and ownership combined with leadership support. By embracing this mindset, there are several benefits that can be expected in terms of performance:

- Inclusive mindset
- Increased adoption
- Instant ownership
- Easier root cause identification

When we think about Open Source Change Management, it includes the following characteristics to be effective:

1. Co-created change strategy with leadership & teams
2. Employee ownership & implementation – empowerment & accountability
3. Regular and ongoing communications that engage the team – "Ask & Talk" not "Sell & Tell"
4. Make experience relevant and specific

5. Build empathy, community and shared purpose across cross-functional teams
6. Demonstrate progress and quick wins – keep people engaged
7. Obtain regular feedback and make adjustments to drive greater ownership and continuous improvement

If it was easy to get from current state to future state, you would see many more successful change initiatives. The path to sustainable change is not rooted in technology, although that can provide support and create new efficiencies. Rather, it is about creating a shared need rooted in your people and the underlying process to better serve your customers while reducing risks and expenses.

To embrace the idea of modern change management, start with the destination in mind. In fact, it will make starting that much easier and will build enthusiasm throughout your organization. Go small starting with one group, one process, one team – don't boil the ocean! Change should be a journey, stay focused on the overall destination and goal. Once you get going, build on that momentum and capitalize on your quick wins to start the domino effect throughout the organization.

Using Analytics to Drive Process Improvement

Change is an essential part of business. Competitors, customers, technology and entire industries are changing rapidly. In business as in life, you either get better or worse but you never stay the same. Sadly, far too many companies are finding this out the hard way. Most companies are often ill equipped to deal with change, let alone proactively execute on it. Amazingly many organizations continue to make the same mistakes over and over again when it is well known that those actions will lead to sub-optimal outcomes. The best way to ensure success is to measure your process using metrics that make sense. This requires you to know your process and how it impacts the enterprise. Start small and build over time. Here are some ways to leverage analytics to drive process improvements:

1. Define exactly what you need to measure
2. Measure what's going on at every stage of your process – critical points, customer touch points and everything that may impact the core deliverables
3. Use analytics to inform process improvements by reviewing data and identifying trends, anomalies and risks
4. Identify areas of improvement or process gaps
5. Put improvements in place and measure again
6. Develop an "early warning" system that will proactively highlight process inefficiencies, risks and gaps
7. Use data to make decisions – easier to justify, track and prioritize

Transformation is never easy to implement while a changing business environment never stops. Using data to transform your business process, engage your people and turn that same process into a strategic asset allows you to tap a never-ending cycle of ingenuity and continuous improvement regardless of industry.

Reflection Point

Think back to a project closely aligned to a particular methodology. How effective was the end result of that project? What worked well and what didn't?

Were you able to use data to reinforce your change? Why or Why not?

Conclusion

There isn't a one size fits all approach to project management. You do not have to be Agile, Lean or Waterfall. You can use the best tools to serve your purpose and ignore the rest. It is not a binary decision. As Bruce Lee said, take what is useful and discard the rest. Tools are just that, tools. They are there to make you better at execution. Project management doesn't have to be complicated, but it is easy to make it arduous. Keep things simple.

In short, it is a simple mindset change to be a leader in successful organizational change. Start with the data you collect and use it to make better decisions and process improvements. Understand how your process really works today and not just how you wished it worked. Collect feedback from multiple sources and empower your teams to build, implement and own the change. Change is never easy and culture change can be even more difficult, but it is never too late to start.

Recommended reading

There isn't one universal manual on project management or process improvement (I wish, that would be awesome!). There are good ideas from many angles and industries. Don't waste your time trying to find the one resource or book of knowledge that will answer all of your questions. The reality is that something like that doesn't exist. That said, the list below represents some of the books that I have found helpful over the years and provided great information.

Thank you for buying this book and hopefully one day you will add it to your own list of recommended reading.

1. Never Split the Difference - by Chris Voss with Tahl Raz
2. Storytelling with Data – A data visualization guide for business professionals – by Cole Nussbaumer Knaflic
3. Why Simple Wins: Escape the complexity trap & get to work that matters – Lisa Bodell
4. Blue Ocean Strategy – W. Chan Kim & Renee' Mauborgne
5. Make Your Bed – Admiral William McRaven
6. Principles – Ray Dalio
7. Make Big Happen – Mark Moses
8. Delivering Happiness – Tony Hseih

Journal

Reflection is critical to make sustainable change. Things will not always go your way, but you can learn from things that do not work or even things that work well. I encourage you to use the pages that follow to document your thoughts, your answers to the reflection points throughout the book or just doodle. Regardless of how you use them, try to learn from the wins and losses over time and apply them to future projects and challenges.

Good luck and remember to keep things simple!

www.ingramcontent.com/pod-product-compliance
Lightning Source LLC
Chambersburg PA
CBHW021410210526
45463CB00001B/296